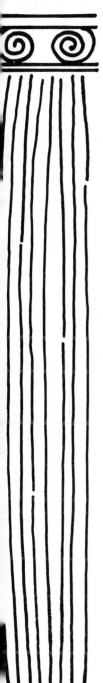

World's Wackiest Lawsuits

K.R. HOBBIE

Illustrated by Lucy Corvino

 Sterling Publishing Co., Inc.   New York

Lawsuit, n.—a machine which you go into as a pig and come out as a sausage.

Ambrose Bierce
The Devil's Dictionary

Edited by Laurel Ornitz

Library of Congress Cataloging-in-Publication Data

Hobbie, K.R.
    World's wackiest lawsuits / K.R. Hobbie ; illustrated by Lucy Corvino.
        p.   cm.
    Includes index.
    ISBN 0-8069-8668-9
    1. Law—United States—Humor.   2. Trials—United States—Humor.
    I. Title.
    K184.H6   1992
    347'.053—dc20   92-18234
    [342.753]   CIP

10   9   8   7   6   5   4   3

Published in 1992 by Sterling Publishing Company, Inc.
387 Park Avenue South, New York, N.Y. 10016
© 1992 by K.R. Hobbie
Distributed in Canada by Sterling Publishing
% Canadian Manda Group, P.O. Box 920, Station U
Toronto, Ontario, Canada M8Z 5P9
Distributed in Great Britain and Europe by Cassell PLC
Villiers House, 41/47 Strand, London WC2N 5JE, England
Distributed in Australia by Capricorn Link Ltd.
P.O. Box 665, Lane Cove, NSW 2066
Manufactured in the United States of America
All rights reserved

Sterling ISBN 0-8069-8668-9

CONTENTS

Introduction   5

1 ■ Oops!   7

2 ■ Sue-ey!   17

3 ■ Road Warriors   31

4 ■ Lights . . . Camera . . . Legal Action!   43

5 ■ There's No Place Like Court   59

6 ■ You Don't Say!   69

7 ■ Boy Sues Girl   79

8 ■ Lawsuits 101   93

9 ■ David v. Goliath   101

10 ■ Three-Piece Suits   113

Index   127

INTRODUCTION

■

How can we call this American book the *World's Wackiest Lawsuits?*
There is some poetic license in our title—but look at the statistics
and you will see that the claim isn't so farfetched.

It's been widely quoted that the United States has 70 percent of
the world's lawyers. Though that figure is almost certainly over-
blown, legal scholars admit that the ratio of lawyers per capita
remains far higher in the U.S. than in other countries.* And
Americans are filing lawsuits at the rate of nearly 18 million a year,
or one for every ten adults. (Have you filed your lawsuit today?)

Much has been written about the ill effects of all this suing:
sky-high liability insurance, doctors running up medical bills
with "defensive" tests, companies afraid to introduce new prod-
ucts, and so on.

Mind you, the right to sue is important in a free country, and
lots of lawsuits are filed for the good reason of protecting someone who was wronged. But when you have 18 million lawsuits,
inevitably a certain number are going to be . . . well, goofy. And
as the nation considers how to accomplish some much needed
legal reform, perhaps a bit of comic relief is not out of place.

The lawsuits in this book have been collected for that purpose.
All these cases are real and a matter of public record. Because our
aim is to amuse, not embarrass, the names of non-public figures
have been changed; but in all other respects, the case descrip-
tions are as accurate as it was possible to make them. (Throughout the book, remarks in quotes are those taken directly from
court records or from one of the parties and remarks not in
quotes have been paraphrased.)

---

*The primary reason America has the lion's share of the world's lawyers,
according to the American Bar Association, is that other countries have too
few.

Some of these cases are amusing because they are so-called "frivolous" suits: When you take your hairdresser to court or sue the band director for not making you drum major, it's going to make people laugh. Thanks to a recent rule, it also may cause the judge to slap you with a frivolous-suit fine. In other cases, it's not the frivolity but the circumstances that are noteworthy: exploding toilets, misplaced navels, pigs that drink beer, computers that insult their owners.

Perhaps one day, when legal restraint has prevailed in the land, we will look back at this lawsuit-happy period in the nation's evolution with a certain nostalgia. The mélange of fuming plaintiffs, indignant defendants, bashed-in fenders, snapping dogs, flying golf balls, and outrageous advertising claims will have become a part of American folklore.

In the meantime, we can surely be forgiven for claiming world-class status in the wacky-lawsuit arena.

■ ■ ■

A warm thank-you to all the attorneys, court clerks, law librarians, and others who helped in the research for this book.

If you have a question about any of the cases—and especially, if you have others to bring to our attention—please write in care of Sterling Publishing Company.

K. R. HOBBIE

1
OOPS!

■

Lawsuits about Accidents

The Case of the "Healing Explosion"

It sounded like the answer to a retired schoolteacher's prayer: a faith-healing session that would finally cure her aching back. And, sure enough, when Ethel got up on stage with the Hill of Faith evangelists, she was so overcome by the "Healing Explosion" that she fainted dead away.

But the evangelists, Herbert and Joy, didn't have their act quite together that day. When Ethel went into her swoon, the designated "catchers" moved in, lunged—and missed. Ethel landed with a crack, fracturing the very spine that everybody was trying to heal.

It was kind of like a doubles tennis match, said the attorney for Hill of Faith; you know, when both players come running and nobody actually connects with the ball? Ethel was not amused. It was the federal court, not the tennis court, that she was interested in.

At the trial, the jury sided with her, ordering Herbert and Joy to fork over $300,000 for their fumble.

The Case of the Terrible Golf Shot

Betty had just putted out at the sixth hole and was standing a few feet from the green when a golf ball came sailing down from regions unknown and conked her right on the head.

The source of the missile: Rudy, located so far from Betty that you wouldn't have guessed there would be any danger. And

there wouldn't, if Rudy hadn't made such a dreadful shot. Rudy's partner, Bob, had even told him that the coast was clear before he took the swing.

Nursing her injured cheekbone, Betty took both Rudy and Bob to court. There, she ran into an unexpected rule of law: the "ambit of danger" rule. If you get beaned by a ball from within a foreseeable danger zone—the area where an onlooker might *reasonably* get beaned—you can collect damages, on grounds that you should have been warned. But if the ball comes at you from far afield, there's nothing you can do.

It came down to how far away Betty was from Rudy and Bob. The judge heard all the arguments—but before the case came to trial, the lawyers decided to take a swing at settling it among themselves.

The Case of the Erupting Toilet

When the septic system goes haywire, no place is safe—not even the executive washroom. That's what Alan, a bank president, discovered as he was sitting on the toilet in the executive washroom in his own bank.

Alan was minding his own business when, suddenly, a geyser of sewage-filled water "came blasting up out of the toilet with such force it stood him right up," as his attorney put it. The geyser ended as quickly as it began—but not before drenching Alan in more than 200 gallons of raw sewage.

This would have been bad enough, but then the press got wind of the story. That was the end of Alan's dignity. So he did what any red-blooded, sewage-soaked businessman would do: sue the building's construction company for damages. There ought to be some compensation, said his attorney, for the "humiliation and embarrassment" Alan suffered as his story seeped all over town.

Alas, the jury, though sympathetic, couldn't be talked into blaming the construction company. Alan was disappointed, but not enough to pump up an appeal.

The Case of the Butchered Ice Cream

Clarence worked in the kitchen of a cruise ship, filling ice cream orders for the ship's waiters. He had scooped his way down to the middle of a 2½-gallon tub one day when he reached a patch of ice cream that was "hard as a brickbat."

Clarence took an 18-inch razor-sharp butcher knife and was chipping away at the icy stuff when the knife slipped. He cut his hand—so badly that he lost two fingers. Inadequate tools to safely perform the task! Clarence cried, and he proceeded to sue the shipping company.

A jury awarded Clarence $17,500, but the Appeals Court reversed the decision. Honestly now, who could have guessed that

Clarence would use a butcher knife to chip the ice cream? the judge reasoned.

The case of the butchered ice cream made it all the way to the U.S. Supreme Court, which found in favor of Clarence after all.

Someone should have transferred the ice cream out of the deep freeze earlier to soften it before serving, the Court ruled. Clarence shouldn't have been stuck with the "totally inadequate" scoop, and, yes, the employer *should* have foreseen that he "might be tempted to use a knife to perform his task with dispatch."

The Case of the Fallen Star

Alice just knew she was going to be a famous opera star. She would dream about it on her way to her singing lessons. She must have been dreaming about it the day she walked through a construction zone—because she stepped right into a hole and fell on her head.

Naturally, Alice sued the construction company. But this wasn't your typical "slip-and-fall" case. Alice sang the blues not just about her fractured leg, but about the bump on her head ... which injured her ear ... which messed up her hearing ... which drove her sense of pitch right out the window.

There wasn't a dry eye in the jury, as Alice, her voice teacher, her opera coach, and her doctor described her tragic fate. Never mind that the young singer hadn't made her debut yet. Never

mind that, according to another doctor, her hearing had been out of whack for years.

The jury awarded Alice $50,000—a mere token compared to the millions she would have made as the next Maria Callas, but still, not bad. However, it was not to be: The construction company appealed and the judge said, Stop the music! Fifty thousand is a mite rich for someone who's got more high hopes than bookings, he told Alice. You can have twenty thousand.

The Case of the Wandering Navel

When he woke up from his cosmetic surgery, Miles discovered some good news and some bad news. The good news was that the bulk had disappeared from his belly. The bad news: There

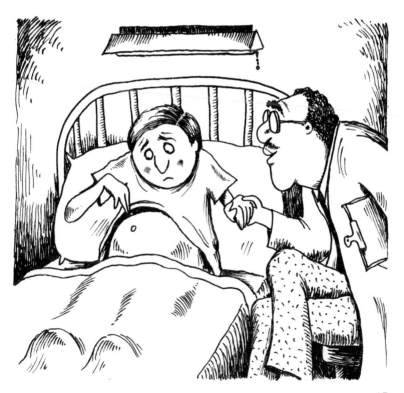

was a big scar there instead—and his belly button wasn't where it was supposed to be.

You never told me this might happen! Miles cried out to Dr. Adam, the plastic surgeon. Miles had gone to see the doctor about a "liposuction" (vacuum-type fat removal), and Dr. Adam had recommended "abdominoplasty" (surgical trimming of fat and skin) as well. According to Miles, there had been no mention of scars or dislocated navels.

So he sued Dr. Adam for negligence. I've suffered "permanent disfigurement, embarrassment, pain of body and mind, and loss of income," he complained. I'm going to need to have this fixed; nobody ought to go through life with his belly button off-center!

Miles wanted a jury trial—but he and Dr. Adam managed to sit down quietly in the waiting room and stitch up their differences themselves.

2

SUE-EY!*

■

Lawsuits about Animals

The Case of the Canine Homeowner

When Violet passed away, she left her $100,000 home to her beloved Skippy, a Pomeranian, to live in for the rest of his life. But this didn't set well with Violet's brothers and sisters. They went to court for permission to sell the house and divide the proceeds. Sorry, said the judge, you'll have to abide by the bequest and wait until Skippy's death.

Three years later, the silver-haired Skippy was still going strong at thirteen years of age—about ninety in human terms—and Violet's heirs went to battle again. How can we be sure some other dog isn't being substituted? they wanted to know, and they demanded that Skippy have his leg tattooed.

That sounded pretty traumatic to Skippy's caretaker, a retired policeman who lived in the basement apartment in the dog's house. Skippy could be identified just as well through X-rays and photographs, he argued.

Once again, the judge found in favor of Skippy. The settlement did allow a detailed inspection of the dog's body to reassure the heirs.

The Case of Bubba, the Beer-Drinking Boar

Bubba was a big, fat, ferocious-looking wild pig—to most people. But to his owners, Clyde and Norma, he was a beloved pet who lived in their backyard and dined on chocolate and beer. They had found Bubba (who looked boar-like but was actually a javelina) on a hunting trip and raised him from babyhood.

All this was in violation of a state law against the keeping of game animals, and the sight of Bubba did startle a neighbor or two. Wildlife officers eventually learned of the matter and came to seize Bubba. Norma got out her shotgun, but to no avail— Bubba was released in a no-hunting area and Clyde and Norma went to trial.

The judge found the couple not guilty of harboring a wild animal, on the grounds that Bubba was no longer "wild." That was a technicality, according to the assistant attorney general. However mild his manner, he said, Bubba was born wild and wild he would always be. But the ruling was enough for Clyde and Norma. They immediately sued for $500,000 for their "pain and suffering."

The District Court judge ruled that Clyde and Norma couldn't collect damages for the loss of Bubba since they had no legal right to him in the first place. But the judge did allow the case to go to trial on a Fourth Amendment issue that had to do with the game wardens illegally walking through the couple's house to the backyard rather than going around it. Yet since Clyde himself had suggested that route, the jury found that it was reasonable for the officers to walk through the house.

Bubba was never seen or heard from after his release, but by that time he had become a big media celebrity. As the assistant attorney general said, "Around here, you've gotta love anybody called 'Bubba'."

The Case of the Slippery Saddle

On vacation at the Rocking Z Ranch, Nancy took a tumble off her horse. She got up, brushed herself off—and filed a product liability suit against the ranch for furnishing her with "defective and dangerous goods."

The ranchers admitted that the horse had a tricky habit of expanding its chest while it was being saddled, which made the saddle tend to wobble sideways. But this was not a dangerous animal, they insisted—"fractious," perhaps, but not dangerous.

The judge agreed. He also nixed Nancy's attempt to classify the matter as a product liability case. A horse and saddle do not constitute a "product," he wrote. "Clearly, no person ever designed, assembled, fabricated (except the Greeks at Troy), produced, constructed, or otherwise prepared a horse."

The Case of the Limping Lovebird

It was mating season, and Lulu the parrot had a hot date with Max at the Bird World aviary. Then suddenly, in the middle of breeding, Lulu turned up one day without three of her toes. The female macaw kept falling off her perch, and amorous activity screeched to a halt.

Lulu's owner, Erik, blamed Bird World. He claimed the aviary was so cold that Lulu had lost her toes to frostbite. But according to the aviary staff, it was more likely that she'd lost them to Max. Breeding parrots often got aggressive enough to bite each other's toes, they said.

Erik wasn't buying that explanation. He'd had big plans for Lulu and Max, whose offspring were supposed to be worth $2,000 apiece. So he filed suit against Bird World for $420,000—including compensatory damages of $170,000 for the eighty-five chicks Lulu might have had.

But the judge wouldn't allow the jury to calculate the chicks-that-might-have-been in their decision-making. Erik—his feathers seriously ruffled—won just $800 for the depreciation in Lulu's value.

The Case of the Cat in the Coffin

Marie, a housewife, was distraught when her pet poodle passed on. She called an animal funeral home, bought a satin-lined casket, and arranged for a proper burial.

But when Marie wanted a last peek before her pet was lowered into the grave, she got the shock of her life. There in the casket, in place of her poodle, was a dead cat.

Marie filed suit, on grounds that she had suffered from "shock, mental anguish, and despondency."

The judge was sympathetic and ordered the vets who had lost track of the poodle to pay Marie $700. In his ruling, the judge endeared himself to animal lovers when he wrote, "A pet is not just a thing, but occupies a special place somewhere in between a person and a piece of personal property."

The Case of the Chain-Link Canines

Lisa was strolling down the sidewalk when she was startled by a pair of dogs leaping and barking loudly behind their chain-link fence. Taken aback, the teenager darted into the street—and was struck a blow by an oncoming car.

Then Lisa struck a few blows of her own. She sued the driver of the car. She sued the owners of the "vicious" dogs. For good measure, she even sued the dog owners' next-door neighbor for not keeping the bushes and shrubs along the sidewalk properly clipped on behalf of pedestrians.

By the time the case reached an appeals court, the driver and the neighbor had been cleared—but Lisa was still trying to bring the dog owners to heel. Sorry, said the appellate judge. "Even if the dogs had been barking or jumping against the fence, such activities are quite common for a dog," he noted. And the idea of keeping a dog completely out of public sight or hearing "offends common sense."

The Case of Grandma's Geese

Everybody knew that Nellie's pet geese had their nasty side. But Mike, Nellie's grandson, wasn't worried the day he dropped by for a visit. He was more concerned about Nellie herself, who was ailing.

When Mike stepped inside the fenced yard, however, the two geese and their three goslings saw red. They rushed at Mike, their necks outstretched. When he turned to run, he tripped and fell, cracking two fingers and a wrist.

When Mike got the doctor bills from his goose attack, it seemed only reasonable to send them to his grandmother's insurance company. No way! said the insurance company. You knew those geese were aggressive, and you assumed the risk when you walked in the gate.

Mike had only one option left: to sue his grandmother for $30,000. No hard feelings, he told Nellie, it's the insurance I'm after. In the end, though, he withdrew his suit, and grandma passed her geese along to a friend.

The Case of the Hen-Pecked . . . er, Parrot-Pecked . . . Husband

City police had a real troublemaker in Anita. Not only did she let her dogs run loose in the park, but she kept on feeding the pigeons there. Sergeant Tom had scolded her twice, and the third time, he issued a citation—or tried to. Anita refused to give her name and address (You know darned well who I am, she said), so the only course left was to arrest her.

Anita's two dogs and the parakeet she "happened to have in hand" wouldn't fit in a jail cell, so Sergeant Tom and Officer Sheila escorted her home first. When Anita's husband, Tony, heard about the arrest, he swore and punched Officer Sheila. Since Tony—and Anita, too—had a reputation as a black-belt karate expert, the officers figured they'd better call for help.

By the time the paddy wagon got there, they had subdued Tony and he was bleeding about the head. I was clobbered by a pair of handcuffs! Tony claimed. You were clobbered by your own parrot, said Sergeant Tom. It landed on your head in the middle of the fight and started pecking.

While the police were hauling Tony to the paddy wagon, Anita locked them out of the house. They had to kick the door in to take her into custody, and Tony and Anita spent the night in jail.

The counts against Anita were severe: littering (dropping bird seed on the ground), feeding birds, allowing her dogs to run unleashed, and resisting arrest. The judge convicted her on the leash charge but let her and Tony off on the rest. Feeding pigeons was okay by the current park rules, he reminded Sergeant Tom, whose rule book happened to be eight years out of date.

Now, it was Tony and Anita's turn. They filed suit for assault, battery, false arrest, and malicious prosecution. A month before the trial, the city offered them $42,000 to settle the matter. That

wasn't enough for Tony and Anita—but it should have been: The jury only awarded them $25,000.

And that wasn't enough for Tony and Anita's lawyers. They wanted nearly $50,000 in fees for the 332 hours they had spent on the case. Ridiculous, said the city. Such a simple case didn't justify all that time (most of which was racked up *after* the settlement offer); the most the lawyers deserved was $5,000. The case went through several appeals before the fee issue finally came home to roost . . . er, rest.

The Case of the Fresh-Baked Rat

Mildred ordered a loaf of bread from her local A&P. When the delivery boy got to her door, he handed her the package and gave her a message from the store manager: "You'd better open it while I am here."

When Mildred opened her package, what she found was not white, whole-wheat, or rye, but a dead rat. In front of the delivery boy's eyes, she fainted and fell "with great force to the floor." In her ensuing lawsuit, Mildred claimed she had suffered "excruciating physical pain and mental anguish."

Evidence showed that the dead rat had been "carelessly substituted" for the loaf of bread by the store manager. (Apparently he had another customer who appreciated such waggish practical jokes.) "I am sorry," he told Mildred's husband, "I sent your wife the wrong package." The court awarded Mildred damages for her injuries and court costs.

3
ROAD WARRIORS

■

Lawsuits about Cars

The Case of the Spy Who Came In from the Trunk

Faced with growing evidence that his wife, Elaine, was having an affair, Chuck decided to check out the matter personally. One night when she was going out, he armed himself with a flashlight and screwdriver and hid in the trunk of her car.

Elaine stopped to pick up her lover, Joe. Then the two parked and moved into the backseat. Chuck leaped out of the trunk and tried to climb into the car to attack his rival. But Joe scrambled out and took the offensive: He hit Chuck on the head, knocked him to the ground, and drove off with Elaine.

When Chuck came to, he found that his wife had abandoned him but his guardian angel hadn't. There on the ground beside Chuck was a pair of men's slacks, which Joe had kicked off the

floor of the car during the struggle. In a pocket was Joe's wallet and ID, along with a handwritten note from Elaine.

In the ensuing divorce case, the judge wrote: "The best of [Elaine's] evidence in denial of the charge is only slightly less incredible than [Joe's] explanation as to how he came to be trouserless in the lady's car."

The Case of the Car in the Creek

Harold was driving his Chevy one winter day when suddenly he spotted another car coming at him in his own lane. He swerved, hit a chunk of ice, skidded into another chunk, and flipped his car—toppling 15 feet down into a gully with an icy stream at the bottom.

When he came to in his upside-down car, Harold saw lots of broken glass and twisted metal, but his own body parts seemed to be in working order. He was, however, in a jam. The car was wedged so tightly in the gully that he couldn't open either door, and the icy stream was gurgling past his ears.

Harold could hear cars passing above him, but blow the horn as hard as he might, he still couldn't make them hear him. He was starting to panic. Then Harold felt an enormous jolt. His car spun around in the creek, and when it stopped—bingo, he was able to open the door!

Sprung from his icy prison, Harold staggered out to see what had happened and discovered that—miraculously—a *second* car had crashed into the creek.

Did Harold fall on his knees and thank the driver, Lucas, for saving his neck? Hardly. Pointing to the back injury he had gotten when the two cars collided, he sued Lucas for $10,000.

A trial judge scoffed at this suit. There wasn't a shred of evidence that Lucas was negligent, he said.

But when Harold appealed his case, he had better luck. Harold had a right to be in that creek, said the Appeals Court judge. He proved he got there through no fault of his own, forced off the road by an oncoming driver. And once he was there, he had a right to peace and quiet.

But what business did Lucas have accidentally landing on top of Harold? Lucas, said the judge, hadn't *proved* he had any more business in the creek than "in a cornfield or in somebody else's front yard."

The Case of the Suspect Belch

When the police saw Scott "driving erratically" one night, they pulled him over. Scott agreed to a breath-alcohol test, and down at the station he got his instructions: No burping, belching, or otherwise "contaminating the oral cavity" for twenty minutes to ensure an accurate test.

The twenty-minute waiting period went by, and Scott stepped

up to the machine—and belched. This meant another twenty-minute wait, said the police, and there'd better not be any more rule-breaking or they'd put Scott down as refusing the test. Fifteen minutes passed. Scott belched again. Shortly after that, he had his license revoked.

I apologize, said Scott, but please—I didn't do it on *purpose!* Anyone would have a tendency to belch after downing a couple of beers and hot dogs, his attorney pointed out. But to the court, Scott's belching smacked of "an attempt to kill time to allow the alcohol to dissipate from his system."

The State Supreme Court agreed. "The question before us is whether a voluntary burp can constitute a refusal to submit to a breath-alcohol test," wrote the judge. The answer: Scott had indeed burped his license away.

The Case of the Low-Gear Lemon

Barely out the showroom door, Paulette began to wonder if buying her brand-new car was such a good idea. The car had gone less than a mile when it stalled at a traffic light. It stalled again after 15 feet—and kept on stalling at every stop sign from then on. Halfway home, Paulette couldn't get the car to run in "drive" at all and called her husband, Cyril, in a panic. Cyril limped the

car home in "low-low." The fastest it would go was 10 miles an hour.

Cyril stomped to the phone and called his bank to cancel the check for the car; then he called the dealer. You sold me a lemon! he cried. The sale's cancelled!

But Randy, the dealer, felt this car was salvageable. He towed it into his shop, replaced the dead transmission with one from a showroom model, and told Cyril: All fixed!

You don't get it, Cyril replied. I don't *want* this car, fixed or no; the sale's cancelled. But Cyril and Paulette still needed a car, and before long they were making a deal with Randy for the next year's model. I'll sell it to you, said Randy, but first we have to "credit" you for the other one. Cyril refused. How many times do I have to tell you that sale was *cancelled*, he said.

Randy wanted the balance he felt Cyril owed him, Cyril wanted his deposit back, and that's how the two wound up in court. We had a signed contract, Randy argued, and that means Cyril "accepted" the car. But the court found that no amount of fine print could make up for a lemon as sour as this one. Every buyer has a right to assume his new car's going to run, the judge noted. When it's "practically inoperable" right out of the showroom and the buyer calls at once to cancel, the deal is definitely off.

The Case of the Runaway Cab

When Ray and Roy pulled a pistol on him in a back alley, Oliver handed over his money. But when the muggers ran off with the loot, Oliver ran off right after them. He was closing in on Roy when the thief spotted a taxicab waiting at the curb and jumped in.

Move! Roy growled to George, the cabdriver, and nudged him with the pistol. George eased the cab into traffic. But he hadn't gone more than 15 feet when he spotted Oliver in hot pursuit in the rearview mirror. Stop! Thief! Oliver was yelling. A little posse of bystanders began running and yelling right along with him. Soon, they were gaining on the slow-moving taxi.

George started to tremble. Do as I say or I'll blow your brains out! Roy snarled. But George had a better idea. Throwing his cab out of gear, he yanked on the emergency brake to send Roy off-balance, flung open the door, and hit the ground running. He was well down the block before he even bothered to look back.

What George saw when he did look back was this: The cab, abandoned by Roy as well, had run up onto the sidewalk and collided with Gladys and her two children. Their injuries were slight, however, and Roy was apprehended, hiding out in the cellar of a nearby hospital.

George thought his troubles were nearly over—until he got a call from Gladys's lawyer. Shame on you for abandoning your cab! We're suing for negligence!, he was told.

Happily for George, the judge had a different idea of negligence. "The test," he pointed out, "is what reasonably prudent men would have done under the same circumstances." And when you're at the point of a gun, he found, the prudent thing is to try and save your own skin. Case dismissed.

The Case of the "Ode on a Damaged Tree"

When a car struck and damaged his "beautiful oak tree," Elsworth was so dismayed that he took the owner of the car and the woman who was driving it to court. He also wanted a judgment against the insurance company covering the vehicle.

Elsworth got nowhere with the trial court. The owner and driver were immune from liability thanks to the state's no-fault insurance act, and the insurance company couldn't be dragged in because Elsworth hadn't gotten the procedure right.

So Elsworth appealed his case. Though the verdict was no different, he did inspire the judge* to write a poetic opinion on behalf of the three-justice panel:

> *We thought that we would never see*
> *A suit to compensate a tree.*

*Judge J. H. Gillis of Michigan.

A suit whose claim in tort is prest
Upon a mangled tree's behest;

A tree whose battered trunk was prest
Against a Chevy's crumpled crest;

A tree that faces each new day
With bark and limb in disarray;

A tree that may forever bear
A lasting need for tender care.

Flora lovers though we three,
We must uphold the court's decree.

4
LIGHTS...
CAMERA...
LEGAL ACTION!

■

Cases
from the World
of Entertainment
and Sports

The Case of the Lost Lottery

Charlene was starting her New Year off with a bang: On December 30, she won $3 million in the state lottery. Five seconds later, she lost it.

In a live telecast, Charlene spun the "Big Spin" wheel and watched open-mouthed as the ball landed in her number. "You're a winner!" shrieked the announcer. The lights flashed and Charlene began to celebrate.

Moments later, the announcer tapped her on the shoulder and told her she wasn't a winner after all. The ball hadn't stayed in the slot for the required five seconds, he said, and all bets were off.

Lottery officials sent Charlene a consolation check for $10,000, but she wasn't giving up her $3 million without a fight. Charlene took the state lottery to court.

During the trial, jury members were shown videotapes of

Charlene's spin and those of other grand-prize winners. What did they find? That although the state might have had a five-second rule, it had never enforced the rule in the past—and there was no reason why it should suddenly do so now. Charlene walked away with her $3 million and another $400,000 for emotional trauma.

The Case of the Warbling Churchgoer

Joanne, a parishioner at Our Lady of Sorrows Catholic Church, had a habit of singing songs that the rest of the congregation wasn't singing. It was bad enough when she sang from her pew, but when she got up and started singing through the sound system, Father Carl resorted to a lawsuit.

Joanne's singing, he said, was causing "confusion and disruption" during church services. In fact, the church had suffered "a loss of good will, spiritual tranquility, and membership."

The judge issued an injunction ordering Joanne to stop the music or risk being held in contempt of court.

The Case of "Fast Eddy," the Accountant

When Edward, an accountant and tax planner, switched on his television April 14, he got a peculiar kind of comic relief. There on "Saturday Night Live," in honor of the next day's income-tax deadline, was a skit about a tax consultant with the same name as his. The performer, Edward felt, even bore a "noticeable physical resemblance" to himself.

But any resemblance to real life ended when SNL's "Fast Eddy" began handing out "advice." Among the highlights:

"Your taxes are due tomorrow. You could wind up with your assets in a sling. So listen closely. Here are some write-offs you probably aren't familiar with—courtesy of 'Fast Eddy.' Got a houseplant? A ficus, a coleus, a Boston fern—doesn't matter. If you love it and take care of it, claim it as a dependent.

"Got horrible acne . . . use a lotta Clearasil? That's an oil-depletion allowance. You say your wife won't sleep with you? You got withholding tax coming back. If she walks out on you, you lose a dependent. But . . . it's a home improvement—write it off.

"Should you happen, while filling out your tax form, to get a paper cut, thank your lucky stars—that's a medical expense and a disability. Got a rotten tomato in your fridge? Frost ruined your crops—that's a farm loss. Your tree gets Dutch elm disease . . . sick leave—take a deduction. Did you take a trip to the bathroom tonight? If you took a trip . . . and you did business—you can write it off.

"Call me. I have hundreds of trained relatives waiting to take your call. At Fast Eddy's, we guarantee your refund will be greater than what you earned."

Edward wrote to the producers, demanding a public apology and compensation. He got only a private apology—and the dubious pleasure of watching Fast Eddy again a couple of months later. That did it, for Edward: He sued the producers and the network for defamation.

But the court found Edward's complaint just as ludicrous as the TV show he was complaining about. The "so-called tax advice" of Fast Eddy, wrote the judge, was "so extremely nonsensical and silly that there was no possibility that any person hearing [it] could take [it] seriously."

The Case of the Suffering Sports Fan

Benjamin, a teacher and coach, was a big tennis fan—but he wasn't a big fan of John McEnroe. And he made it abundantly clear one August day when he was seated courtside at a preliminary round of the U.S. Open.

Not only was Benjamin rooting openly for McEnroe's opponent, but he was cheering each time McEnroe made a fault. "Don't you have anything better to do than cheer for my opponent all afternoon?" the tennis star cried. "No!" said Benjamin, and McEnroe shouted an obscenity back.

Tempers rose until finally McEnroe strode over to Benjamin, launched into a verbal tirade, and flung his racket in the air. Then, trailing a cloud of rosin from the racket, McEnroe stalked back and resumed play. He won his match three sets to two.

A week later, he faced a $6 million lawsuit.

Benjamin claimed he'd suffered "grievous physical and mental injuries." But that was putting it a bit strongly, according to the judge. McEnroe's behavior was "shabby" and "childlike" but hardly intolerable, he found. Far from assault and battery, the worst Benjamin had suffered was a fleck or two of rosin drifting in his direction. The judge dismissed the complaint.

The Case of the Bad Polish Jokes

The movie *Flashdance* had one Polish joke too many for Anna. She decided it was time to stand up for her heritage where it counted—in court.

Anna filed a class action suit against Paramount Studios on grounds of defamation, infliction of emotional distress, and infringement of Polish people's civil rights. She didn't want any damages, since she'd only suffered "psychic injury"; Anna was suing on principle, not for money. And she turned down court-appointed attorneys in favor of representing herself.

The judge studied each of Anna's theories but found her case "couldn't be salvaged" under any of them. "At worst, the 'Polish jokes' in *Flashdance* indirectly disparaged the intelligence of Polish-Americans and thereby injured their general reputation in the community," he allowed.

The Case of the Cartoon Strip-Tease

The videocassette was clearly labelled "Care Bears Storybook," but that's not what was on the tape—as Karen discovered after her four-year-old had watched the whole thing. Instead of a cartoon about teddy bears, little Sally had just witnessed a Playboy striptease.

Mind you, there *were* cartoons involved: The *Playboy Farmer's Daughters* video featured nude dancers with overlays of cartoon farm animals as the cheering section. But this wasn't the kind of cartoon that Karen had had in mind.

Now, Sally wanted to dance like "the Care Bears video with the naked ladies." She was even telling her friends at school about it.

Karen called Blockbuster Video and let them have it. We're

sorry, but it's beyond our control, said the store; but we'll give you ten free videos to make up for it.

That wasn't enough for Karen. She sued Blockbuster for "negligence and emotional distress." I want "medical and/or counselling expenses" for Sally, said Karen, and I want you to pre-screen all children's videos before renting them out.

To Blockbuster, this was taking a simple mix-up way too far. The judge agreed.

The Case of the Ten-Foot Tomato

When you're stuck with a giant metal tomato on the roof of your restaurant and you want to change your image, what do you do with the tomato? Pasquale's Restaurant came up with a great idea: Hold a contest and *award* it to somebody.

Alex and a bunch of his friends were dining out at Pasquale's. On a lark, Alex entered the contest to win the tomato by guessing its weight. He wrote "555 pounds" on a slip of paper, popped it in the slot, and forgot all about it.

So it came as a bit of a surprise some weeks later when Rich, the owner of Pasquale's, drove up to Alex's house with the giant tomato on a flatbed truck. It seems that Alex had come within 5 pounds of the exact weight. Since he didn't have space for the thing—it was 5 feet tall and 10 feet around—the two agreed to put it in storage.

The tomato made its way to the home of John, an employee of the restaurant. Before long, John began to stew. He claimed his employer owed him money for "expenses incurred" in storing the tomato.

Alex, meanwhile, was getting phone calls from people who actually wanted to buy the tomato. When one party offered $200, Alex agreed and he sent her to Rich, who sent her to John. The buyer got frustrated at this runaround, and Alex got mad. He filed suit against Rich. Rich filed suit against John.

Fed up, the judge ordered John to return the killer tomato to the restaurant. When the restaurant returned it to Alex, he dropped his suit—and promptly sold the tomato.

The Case of the Battling Baked Goods

It was a tense moment in the bakery big leagues. The Pillsbury Doughboy, TV commercial star, was going head to head with Drox, the Hydrox cookie character, in a trademark infringement suit.

In spite of his giggles and excess weight, the Doughboy was a tough contender. Pillsbury had created him to market its rolls, and the Doughboy had been rising nicely to the occasion for more than twenty-five years. Drox was the brainchild of Sunshine Biscuits, Inc. The creamy little character came to life on TV from the filling of Hydrox cookies.

The two coexisted in peace until Drox got a facelift—and began looking a little too much like the Doughboy, according to Pillsbury. So Pillsbury filed suit (for an undisclosed amount of dough), and for a time it appeared that Drox and the Doughboy might actually slug it out in court.

But a last-minute settlement saved the day. Sunshine agreed to drop Drox (without admitting trademark infringement), and Pillsbury agreed to drop its suit.

The Case of the Out-of-Bounds Ball Game

Kermit and his friends were playing softball in the city park when a police officer called time-out. This is a hardball field—no softball allowed, said the policeman, pointing to the sign.

But Kermit wouldn't go. Cite me! he said, so the policeman wrote up a citation. Kermit refused to sign it, and the policeman had to arrest him.

A freshly minted law school grad, Kermit knew just what to do next. I'm suing for damages! he declared. You violated my First, Fourth, and Fourteenth Amendment rights!

That softball game, Kermit argued, wasn't just sport—it was "symbolic speech." He and his friends were "making a statement about the right to democracy in recreation as opposed to elitism." The city, he claimed, had no business restricting softball to one area and hardball to another. Why, such an "arbitrary and invidious" distinction was downright unconstitutional.

Oh, no, it wasn't, ruled the judge. It was for perfectly good safety reasons. As for Kermit's freedom of speech, he noted, what's the "message" inherent in a softball game? And if there were one, how would anybody get it? Go "convey your message" on the softball field, the judge told Kermit. You just struck out!

The Case of the Bulky Coats

Marshall, an attorney, knew how to celebrate his thirty-fifth birth-day in style: at the chic Skye View Restaurant atop the city's tallest office tower. While he and his friends were waiting to be seated, the host told Marshall he'd have to check his raincoat. Marshall said he'd rather keep it with him, but the host insisted: It was restaurant policy that gentlemen check their coats.

Only gentlemen—not ladies? asked Marshall, his ears pricking up. Only gentlemen, said the host. That was all Marshall needed to hear. He marched his friends out of the restaurant and filed a sex-discrimination complaint.

The restaurant claimed its policy was a "legitimate business judgment." We're not trying to discriminate against men, said the owners, but when you hang a bulky coat over the back of your chair, it gets in people's way. If it falls on the floor—heavens, somebody could trip over it and get hurt. And everyone knows that men's coats are bulkier than women's.

Sez you, argued Marshall. Everyone knows that *women's* coats are bulkier than *men's*.

After hearing both sides, the judge decided that men were getting a bum deal at Skye View and he ordered the restaurant to "cease and desist" its one-sided coat policy. He wouldn't, however, give Marshall the damages he wanted for "mental anguish."

5
THERE'S NO PLACE LIKE COURT

■

Lawsuits Involving the Home

The Case of the Smoke-Filled Rooms

Hilary, a cigarette smoker, didn't mind the no-smoking rules at work—but it was a different matter when a neighbor took her to court for smoking in her own home.

Stanley, whose apartment was directly above Hilary's, complained that the smoke from her cigarettes was oozing up through vents and cracks and driving him crazy. So, he filed a nuisance suit.

Hilary admitted to a certain amount of smoking: up to six cigarettes a day, she told the judge. But could this possibly be an "illegal activity" in her own home? The lease, she pointed out, didn't say a word about it.

Not having any hard evidence about the volume of smoke in Stanley's apartment, the judge dismissed his suit as so much hot air. The smoke from a few cigarettes, he ruled, was hardly "an annoyance of a real and substantial nature."

The Case of the Nine-Hole Nuisance

Cracked windows and dents in the car were par for the course for Sylvia and her family. They lived alongside a city-owned, par-three golf course—and the duffers who played there were wreaking havoc on their lives.

Sylvia's backyard was less than 50 yards from the green on the third hole. By the time she decided to go to court, Sylvia had an impressive handicap: twenty-two dents in the family cars, three shattered windshields, and seven broken windows in the house and garage.

Sylvia won her civil suit. The judge gave her $2,500 for property damage and $3,700 for disruption of her "quietude of domicile." But he wouldn't rule the golf course a public nuisance, and the slices and hooks continued to rain golf balls onto Sylvia's property.

Sylvia made one last stab at restoring her family's peace. She tried to get criminal charges filed against the city for 1,087 counts of reckless endangerment and 1,087 counts of criminal trespass by people and golf balls—one count for each golf ball in the four-year family collection. But it didn't work. On this claim, the court told Sylvia, you're out of bounds.

The Case of the Haunted Home Buyer

Guy, a former city dweller, had signed the papers, deposited $32,500—and was looking forward to village life. The historic town was rich in folklore, including a few "haunted" houses. What Guy didn't realize was that one of those houses was his.

Guy's first clue came when his architect refused to work on the place, on grounds that it was ghost-ridden. Then he discovered what Penelope, the seller, had failed to mention: that a round-cheeked little wraith in revolutionary dress had been hanging around the house for years.

Penelope had written all about it in the local papers and the *Reader's Digest*. The ghost was perfectly cheerful, she reported. The worst it had done was eat a ham sandwich.

But Guy wasn't about to pay $650,000 to share his ham sandwich. Cancel the sale! he cried. I want my deposit back! And he sued both Penelope and the realtor.

Was Guy's ghost real? It didn't matter, the Appeals Court found. The fact that Penelope made the story public meant that "as a matter of law, the house is haunted." Its eerie reputation affected both its value and its resale potential, the court ruled, and Guy had a right to know about that.

What about "caveat emptor," or buyer beware? argued the defense. That was the going rule in real estate transactions (and a uniquely appropriate phrase in this case).

It is up to the buyer to find any problem conditions through a "reasonable inspection of the premises," the court noted. But in a case like this, as the judge put it, "Who you gonna call?" Do you take a psychic along with the structural engineer and the termite man on every home inspection? The very notion, the court ruled, should be "laid quietly to rest."

The Case of the Poolside Cemetery

Gilbert and Denise should have had grave misgivings about their new home. Somebody had told the builder that there was an old cemetery on the site and showed him a little fenced-in area with a cross on a stick. Maybe a dog's grave, the builder thought, and he had the debris hauled off and dumped.

It wasn't till two years later, when they decided to put in a swimming pool, that Gilbert and Denise first heard of the matter. Better put a good lining in that pool, warned a neighborhood old-timer. Rumor has it there's a body or two in your backyard.

Sure enough, when they checked it out, the couple learned that there had once been a graveyard on their land. So they put the chlorine on hold and called the excavator instead.

Two human graves turned up. The developer had them moved to a cemetery, but Gilbert and Denise weren't about to let this matter rest in peace. They filed suit for damages, for a host of violations including breach of contract, negligence, and fraud.

Our lives aren't the same since we found those graves, said Gilbert and Denise. We can't sleep, we've lost weight . . . and it's creepy around here! A jury awarded them $142,600. But the trial judge took it back. That cemetery was abandoned, which means your complaints are moot, said the judge—and the Appeals Court.

The State Supreme Court, though, breathed life back into the case. Just because a graveyard isn't a *working* graveyard anymore doesn't mean the poor homeowners have to put up with it, the court found. Gilbert and Denise did deserve a remedy.

The Case of the Unmowed Lawn

But we're making hay! said Kevin and Anne when their neighbors complained about their 2-foot-high front lawn. They planned to mow the grass, honest they did, said the couple. They just wanted to wait until fall, when the harvest would be mature.

That wasn't good enough for their neighbor, Darrell. Darrell and his wife had their house on the market, and the untidy mess at Kevin and Anne's was creating the wrong ambience. In fact, Darrell felt that the two grass lovers were deliberately out to sabotage his real estate sale. So he sued them for $2.5 million.

When the case reached County Court, the judge burst out laughing and dismissed the complaint. But, as a consolation to Darrell, he ordered Kevin and Anne to cut their grass by the first of September.

That's not fall! argued the couple's attorney. Said the judge: "Fall is going to come earlier this year."

The Case of the Weed Invasion

Weeds in the yard were one thing, but when the weeds came poking through the floor in their brand-new home, Terry and Ruth called a lawyer. They'd been in their $80,000 rambler for about a year when horsetail weeds began coming up through the seams where the floors met the walls in every room of the house.

Terry and Ruth complained to the builder. He took measures to get rid of the problem, but the horsetails were stubborn as mules. Terry and Ruth were still hard at work weeding the garage at the time they decided to file suit.

The builder hadn't prepared the ground properly before pouring the slab floor, they argued, and that was how the weeds got a foothold. We want out of here! said the couple. But by the time the case reached court three years later, the judge ruled the house "habitable" and found in favor of the builder.

The Case of the Falling Acorns

Those pesky acorns that kept dropping from their neighbor's oak tree were a serious problem to Mac and Margaret. The darned things came down like a hailstorm, coating the driveway and sidewalks. A body could slip and break his neck.

Mac and Margaret complained to the neighbor, Calvin, time and again: Cut down the part that hangs over our property, they begged. You cut it down, said Calvin. Finally the elderly couple had no choice but to sue. They took Calvin to court for "an unspecified amount of damages" and to force him to trim his tree.

That was enough to get Calvin and his chainsaw into action, and the suit was settled out of court.

6
YOU DON'T SAY!

■

Libel, Slander, and Privacy Lawsuits

The Case of the Rotten Restaurant Review

"T'aint Creole, t'aint Cajun, t'aint French, t'aint country American, t'aint good." That's how Fritz, the food critic, began his review of the new restaurant Maison de Marvin.

In his newspaper column, Fritz went on at great length about how much he didn't like this restaurant. The oysters Bienville were "a ghastly concoction," the escargots à la Marvin "pretentious failures that leave a bad taste in one's mouth." "The poached trout under crawfish sauce," he wrote, "I would have named trout à la green plague."

As for the roast duck: "Put a yellow flour sauce on top of the duck, flame it for drama, and serve it with some horrible multi-flavored rice in hollowed-out fruit, and what have you got? A well-cooked duck with an ugly sauce that tastes too sweet and thick and

makes you want to scrape off the glop and eat the plain duck." Fritz later called this dish "yellow death on duck."

"A travesty of pretentious amateurism. ... I find it all quite depressing," Fritz summed up. "Only the proprietor can answer the question of whose taste is on the menu. If it is his, then this restaurant is an irremediably ghastly mistake."

Having his restaurant labelled a ghastly mistake was too much for Chef Marvin, and he sued for $2 million. You've injured my professional reputation, lost me business, and personally humiliated me, he told Fritz and his newspaper.

The review wasn't malicious, said Fritz, it was simply "fair comment." When a lower court agreed with that, Marvin appealed—but didn't do any better. Though one dissenting judge did call the review "a degrading, malicious, and unprovoked attack," the court ruled that "ordinary reasonable persons" would see it merely as "expressions of the writer's opinion."

The Case of the "Careless" Accident Victim

Little Becky was hit by a car in a street accident in her hometown. A newspaper photographer on the scene got a dramatic shot of the ten-year-old being lifted to her feet, and the picture ran in the next day's paper. The driver was found at fault in the accident, and Becky recovered from her injuries.

She and her family got a second shock, though, when they opened their *Saturday Evening Post* a year and a half later. There was the picture of Becky, illustrating a feature story titled "They Ask to Be Killed." The story, on the theme of pedestrian carelessness, included this splashy blurb: "Do you invite massacre by your own carelessness? Here's how thousands have committed suicide by scorning laws that were passed to keep them alive."

This was too much for Becky and her family. They sued the publisher (who, as it happened, had bought the photo from a supplier of illustration material). A lower court awarded the family $5,000 for their pains, and an appeals court upheld the ruling. The original use of the photo was fine, the judge found. It had legitimate news value at that time. But its use in the *Post* did "exceed the bounds of privilege."

The Case of the Flyaway Skirt

Frieda, a middle-aged farmer's wife, never guessed she'd be the local pin-up girl when she took her two children to the county fair. But a hired photographer snapped a photo of Frieda in the fun house with her skirt blown up over her waist—and the local paper ran the photo on page one.

A lifelong resident of the county and a pillar of her church, Frieda was shocked when she spotted the paper on a display rack and chagrined when several of her friends mentioned it. She sued for invasion of privacy, claiming that the incident had made her "embarrassed, self-conscious, and upset" and that she "was known to cry [about it] on occasions."

The court found that Frieda's privacy had indeed been breached and awarded her damages. "We can see nothing of legitimate news value in the photograph," the judge ruled. "Certainly it discloses nothing as to which the public is entitled to be informed."

The Case of the Missing Bottle Box

As part of her hotel lobby newsstand, Genevieve sold Coca-Cola from a vending machine. A Coke employee would drop by regularly to take away the empty bottles and bring refills.

One midsummer day, Genevieve noticed that she was missing an empties box and "politely inquired" about it. Rick, the Coke

man, replied "in a burst of explosive anger and in a loud and menacing voice." "You've got that case back there in the corner! I can see it from here!" he yelled.

Genevieve tried to explain that there was no empties box in the corner. She even offered to show him. But Rick would have none of it. "I don't have to go back there," he said. "You know you've got that box back there. You fool with me and I'll take that box out of here!"

Since this tiff was taking place in full view of customers, hotel workers, and "the public in general," Genevieve got so upset that she decided to sue the Coca-Cola Bottling Company—for slander. But the court let the fizz out of Genevieve's complaints. The incident, it ruled, was "at most . . . one of those stupid, unnecessary, and ill-tempered arguments which, if they should be held as constitutional slander . . . would overburden the courts."

The Case of the Purloined Porter

Cole Porter has been swiping my tunes for just about long enough, Lenny decided—and he sued the famous songwriter for copyright infringement. It wasn't Lenny's first lawsuit, not by a long shot. Over the years, he'd sued five other composers for the same offense.

Cole Porter hadn't dreamed up "My Heart Belongs to Daddy" all by himself, Lenny claimed. The tune came from Lenny's "A Mother's Prayer." "Begin the Beguine" came from there, too. "Night and Day" was stolen from Lenny's "I Love You Madly," and "Don't Fence Me In" was right out of "A Modern Messiah."

Lenny wanted "at least $1 million out of the millions Cole Porter is earning out of all the plagiarism." When the judge asked Lenny where Porter might have heard his music in order to copy from it, Lenny pointed out that "A Mother's Prayer" had sold more than a million copies. As for the other pieces, most of them had been played at least once over the radio.

Besides, Lenny claimed, Cole Porter "had stooges right along to follow me, watch me, and live in the same apartment with me." His room had been ransacked several times, he said. How do you know Cole Porter had anything to do with it? the judge asked. "I don't know that he had anything to do with it; I only know that he *could* have," Lenny explained.

The district judge found Lenny's whole story fantastic and dismissed it. The Appeals Court, though, did find similarities between Lenny's music and Cole Porter's. Yes, the judge admitted, that part about the stooges was pretty weird, but "sometimes truth is stranger than fiction." It would be up to a jury to decide.

Sadly for Lenny, the jury didn't swallow his story. He appealed again—he even petitioned the U.S. Supreme Court—but finally he had to compose himself and go home.

The Case of the Vengeful Newspaper

When Virginia saw what the *Gazette* had printed, she was so mad she could hardly see straight. There were the profiles of all the candidates for the upcoming election, but the profile of her candidate, Kay, was garbled to the point where it made no sense.

I don't think this was completely accidental, Virginia said to herself. These guys were out to get my candidate! So she wrote an angry letter to the editor of the *Gazette*. To make sure her letter would run in full, she asked that it be published as a paid ad and she sent the paper a check for $560. The *Gazette* printed Virginia's letter. Then it turned around and sued her for libel and slander.

"A man-bites-dog story!" said the Appellate judge when the case reached his court. Nobody had ever heard of a newspaper suing over its own contents. A trial judge had ruled that this couldn't be done—but the *Gazette* appealed, on grounds that Virginia had "compelled" it to print her ad.

Nobody compelled anybody, the Appeals Court found. The

Gazette had freely chosen to publish Virginia's statements. And as the publisher, it couldn't sue, because "it is self-axiomatic that a person cannot sue himself or herself."

7
BOY SUES GIRL

■

Love, Marriage, and Divorce Court

The Case of the Buttock-Biting Barrister

When Ted spotted Susie in a barroom near the university, he was so overcome by her charms that he grabbed her by the hips and gave her a bite on the backside. I meant it as a compliment! Ted claimed. As a lawyer, he should have known better. Ted soon found himself on the receiving end of a lawsuit.

The amorous bite, said Susie's attorney, broke the skin on her buttocks and caused "searing and throbbing pain." Susie couldn't even attend classes—she couldn't sit down for three days.

Ted admitted to nipping his victim, but he insisted he meant her no harm. He had already tried the technique on two other women at fraternity parties, and neither of them took him to court.

This time, however, the victim bit back. While Ted and his lawyer felt that Susie deserved only the $9 she spent on medication, the jurors awarded her $27,500 in damages.

The Case of the Squatter's Rights

His marriage was only a month old, but Billy was ready to call it quits. The ceremony shouldn't have happened in the first place, he claimed in his divorce petition: He was drunk on more than 2 gallons of beer at the time, and when he got cold feet, his 230-pound bride sat on him.

Pleading with the court to dissolve the union on grounds of "cruel and inhuman treatment," Billy claimed that his wife, Cissie, knew darned well he was drunk when she sat on him. There was an argument, he said, during which Cissie knocked him to the ground, sat on him, and "would not allow him his freedom" for a good ten minutes.

I did not knock him down! Cissie countered. He stumbled and fell, and I sat on his lap. Then I told him he wasn't getting up unless we went through with it.

The judge went through with the divorce.

The Case of the Ousted Spouse

In the midst of divorce proceedings, Carol felt she couldn't tolerate Gerald's presence in their Manhattan apartment for one more minute. So she had the locks changed.

Normally, a divorce court wouldn't allow her to get away with such a move, since Gerald wasn't physically abusive. But Carol argued a different form of abuse.

Gerald hadn't taken a bath or changed his clothes in weeks, she pointed out. In a 450-square-foot studio apartment, that was cause for drastic action. The judge agreed. "There is no reason why the plaintiff should be subjected to the extremely uncomfortable situation that prevailed prior to defendant being locked out," he sniffed.

The Case of the Drop-In Husband

Hugh and Connie were separated . . . sort of. Hugh had moved out, but he made a habit of dropping by for dinner and some after-dinner wifely attention. Then he'd ride off into the sunset.

After three-and-a-half years of this, Connie got fed up. I'm too old for "one-night stands," she told Hugh; dinner is all you're getting from now on. Hugh promptly sued for divorce—on grounds that his wife had "abandoned" him.

The court, however, wouldn't buy this logic. You can't abandon someone who's already moved out, the judge told Hugh. Connie was perfectly justified in feeling uncomfortable with the arrangement and putting an end to it. After three-and-a-half years, there was plainly no reconciliation in the works. Hugh, ruled the court, just wanted to "continue his nocturnal comings and goings."

The Case of the Skinflint Widow

When she got the bill for her late husband's funeral, Eliza dug in her heels. They'd been separated at the time of Jake's death, she said, so she had no obligation to pay. This reasoning had not, of course, stopped her from collecting Jake's life insurance.

The undertaker sued, and the case made its way to the State Supreme Court. There, the puzzled judge found no specific law on the books to cover such situations. He had to rely on common law to find that, though a husband was responsible for his wife's funeral expenses, she was not for his.

"It regretfully appears," he noted, "that the undertakers who performed the last earthly service for Jake will have to look to a greater court than this for their reward."

The Case of the Split Windfall

Beverly was faithful to the state lottery. She bought a ticket every week, and every now and then she would win a little. Burt thought she was silly. In his view, the lottery was a waste of money that they should be saving to buy a house.

He did make one exception: When his co-workers decided to spring for some lottery tickets through an office pool, Burt went along. He knew if he refused and they won, Beverly would be hopping mad.

As it happened, the office pool *did* win. In fact, Burt and his buddies won the grand prize. But Beverly was hopping mad anyhow. You see, it wasn't long after Burt's big win that the couple split up—and Burt demanded the lion's share of the lottery winnings.

A trial court sided with Burt, giving him 85 percent of the loot

and Beverly a paltry 15 percent. When she appealed, though, Beverly's luck began to change.

The winning ticket was purchased with "marital funds," the Appeals Court found, and should be shared equally since Burt and Beverly shared equally in the costs of their household.

Burt said he deserved more because he'd gone to the trouble of buying the ticket. As for "marital funds," he claimed, the dollar he used to buy the ticket "might have been a dollar I found on the street the day before while walking the dog."

Sorry, said the court, your winnings were more a matter of good fortune than of anyone's special efforts. And after Beverly had deposited her "meager" winnings into the joint account for all those years, it was only fair for Burt, too, to share and share alike.

The Case of the Nagging Wife

After almost forty years of marriage, Lee was breaking loose. First he found a new love, Doreen; then he moved out on the old one, Roberta.

Roberta asked the court for alimony. The separation, she pointed out, was the fault of the two-timing Lee. But Lee argued that it was just as much Roberta's fault. Her constant henpecking all those years made it plain impossible to stay married to her, he said.

Roberta's "harassment, accusations, and nagging" amounted to such "cruel treatment" that living with her was "insupportable," Lee claimed. He had a witness testify that Roberta was rude to him in public, made scenes about his affair with Doreen, and even called him "bald-headed."

That sounded pretty serious to the trial court and the Appeals Court. Both of them agreed with Lee that the breakup was partly Roberta's fault, which meant that she wasn't eligible for alimony. But the State Supreme Court found that Lee was taking a little nagging way too far.

"All spouses have faults," the court pointed out. And Roberta's faults, it found, were hardly so cruel or excessive that Lee was compelled to leave. After all, he "had tolerated his wife's tongue for nearly forty years," hadn't he?

The Case of the Missing Funds

After she married Myron, Roxanne went to work as bookkeeper of his company, Wilson Widgets. Three years later, she wanted the job but not the husband. Roxanne filed for divorce but kept on at Wilson Widgets . . . until Myron began to suspect that his bookkeeper was making off with the funds.

You're through, Myron told Roxanne. By now she had opened a catering business on the side. But profits were poor. Roxanne claimed that she had only $140 in the bank when she went to court seeking temporary maintenance.

Myron's got more than a million bucks; why shouldn't I have some? Roxanne asked the court, and she won $2,500 a month plus costs. But Myron blew the whistle on that. We haven't cleared up the matter of Wilson Widgets' missing funds, he reminded the Appeals Court.

Myron had a fistful of documents pointing to Roxanne as the "thief"—documents totaling more than $25,000. But when his lawyer asked Roxanne about it, she pleaded the Fifth Amendment. I have the right not to incriminate myself, said Roxanne, and I'm keeping my mouth shut.

That *was* her privilege, the court agreed, but it put Roxanne in a "Catch-22." If she wanted support, she had to fess up about how much money she really had; if she wanted to plead the Fifth, it disqualified her for support. That's the rule, said the court.

Maybe in a really *serious* case, like murder, Roxanne argued, but for a silly little embezzlement? Why, my case "pales in comparison." The rule's the rule, said the court.

The Case of the Costly Non-Divorce

Sure, I'll handle your divorce for you, Nathan told Meg. Here's how it works: You pay me a retainer of $15,000 to cover all the work I'm going to do. And, by the way, that $15,000 is nonrefundable.

Meg went along with it. But as luck would have it, soon after she signed the agreement, love conquered all and Meg decided to stay married. I don't need you anymore, she told Nathan.

According to his billing records, Nathan had spent a total of five hours on Meg's case. At $275 an hour, she figured she owed him $1,305 and she wanted the rest back. Sorry! said Nathan. Don't you remember what I said about "nonrefundable"?

At that, Meg filed suit against her lawyer. And though Nathan claimed that his agreement was perfectly ethical, the court found otherwise.

Discounting the first eight-tenths of an hour that Nathan billed Meg because it occurred before the agreement was even signed, the court found that he was charging her what amounted to $3,571.43 an hour. A fee that high was so "grossly excessive" that it was "shocking to the court's conscience."

There's no way this agreement is enforceable, the court told Nathan. On top of that, it discourages your client's absolute right to discharge you, and it doesn't exactly encourage her to reconcile, either. Give the money back, plus interest!

8
LAWSUITS 101

■

Cases from School and College

The Case of the Drummed-Out Musician

Jerry was first-chair saxophone in his high school marching band, but he had a splashier role in mind. In his senior year, Jerry went out for drum major. He made it to the finals, but he wasn't chosen—and by this time, all the slots in the saxophone section were full.

You can play the cymbals till marching season is over, said Sam, the band director. Then you can be a saxophonist again.

This was small comfort to Jerry. In fact, the thought of cymbal-banging made him so mad that he marched into County Superior Court and filed a complaint against Sam. Not choosing me as drum major was a violation of my constitutional rights, Jerry argued.

And not letting me go back to first-chair saxophone—that was a violation of my constitutional rights, too!

But the judge saw the matter of rights a little differently. It's the band director's right to choose who plays what, the judge ruled, and he sent Jerry marching out the door.

The Case of the Teacher's Kick-Back

All was well on the preschool playground except that little Timmy wouldn't put his bicycle away. Timmy's teacher, Jenny, asked him once and the five-year-old just ignored her. When she asked him again, he threw a tantrum.

While Jenny was trying to calm Timmy down, he turned and kicked her so hard in the ankle that she fell on the ground. And that was the incident that caused Jenny to strike a blow for pre-school teachers everywhere: She filed suit against Timmy and his parents for $25,000.

Timmy's kick, as it turned out, packed such a wallop that Jenny was off work for months and had to have a series of operations to correct her "tarsal tunnel syndrome." For a long time, she could walk only with the aid of a cane.

There's a happy ending, though. The case was settled out of court, Jenny hobbled back to the classroom, and Timmy graduated from preschool and awaits a bright future in the NFL.

The Case of the Would-Be Doctor

Patience was a nurse with a mission: to go to medical school and become a doctor. A thorough person, she applied to every medical school in her state. All seven turned her down. It wasn't that Patience was a terrible candidate—but she wasn't a terrific one, either. "There were at least 2,000 unsuccessful applicants who had better academic qualifications," said the dean of one of the medical schools.

Then Patience discovered her true calling: not medicine, but the law. She promptly filed suit against two of the schools that had rejected her, alleging (among other things) age and sex discrimination. Her case made its way to the U.S. Supreme Court and back, to no avail.

Four years later, she sued the other five schools, with no better luck. And five years after that, Patience took all seven medical schools back to court, on somewhat different legal theories but with the same underlying facts.

Give up! said the weary judge. He dismissed the case, awarded fees and costs to the defendants—and scolded Patience's attorney for not recognizing "an obviously lost cause."

The Case of the Lost .065

As the salutatorian of her high school class, Shelly took her grade-point average seriously ... very seriously. One day she missed algebra class. Since she had no excuse, the teacher lowered her grade—and that meant a slip in her overall grade-point average from 95.478 to 95.413.

Now, .065 might not sound like much; but to Shelly's dad, Ralph, you start letting the little things go and pretty soon the big ones will follow. Ralph saw only one solution: to sue the school board for a million dollars.

That docked grade-point was a violation of his daughter's Fifth and Fourteenth Amendment rights, Ralph told the court. The judge consented to the reinstatement of the grade-points, but he refused to award any money. Ralph appealed the decision, hoping at least to get his attorney's fees paid—but the Appeals Court judge was so exasperated he took the grade-points away again. "Patently insubstantial" was how the judge saw this case.

9
DAVID V. GOLIATH

■

The Little Guy Sues the Big Guy—
and Vice Versa

The Case of the Forty Billion Burgers

Matthew and Nicole passed the golden arches every day—but one day, the big sign made them do a double-take. Could McDonald's really have sold "more than 40 *billion*" hamburgers? Matthew asked Nicole. Let's figure it up, she replied.

According to Nicole's calculations, McDonald's would have had to sell a hamburger every second of every day for a thousand years to reach that number. They would have had to kill every cow born since the 1600s.

Aha! the two exclaimed. False advertising! And they filed suit against McDonald's.

We want the U.S. government to stop McDonald's from lying to the public, Matthew and Nicole argued. "Lies cause great mental strain on the individual as well as the nation," they explained. And we want the IRS to substantiate this claim about the forty billion

burgers, they added. Come up with an income statement and we'll drop our suit—and "throw ourselves on the fairness of the Court to give us a fair percentage of the money uncollected in tax."

Alas, Matthew and Nicole came up empty-handed. The court dismissed their suit, deciding instead: You deserve a break today, McDonald's.

The Case of the Accountant's Birthday Suit

The IRS was on the trail of Craig, a self-employed accountant. Craig had hundreds of thousands of dollars in unaccounted-for bank deposits—deposits on which he had paid no income tax. After

years of pursuit involving records from twenty different bank and brokerage accounts, the U.S. Tax Court finally hauled Craig in.

Craig had dozens of reasons why his deposits weren't taxable income, including one $537 item that struck the Tax Court as particularly "novel." This $537 is obviously a gift, Craig claimed. It has to be, because I put it into the bank on my *birthday.*

Many happy returns, said the court—tax returns, that is.

The Case of the Too-Many Taj Mahals

When your name is Trump, you've got to spend a certain amount of time defending that name from misuse. "The Donald"* was no stranger to the courts. But he wasn't used to being on the receiving end of the lawsuit—and that's just where he was when Victor decided he didn't want any more Taj Mahals cluttering up the marketplace.

Victor ran a second-floor Indian eatery called the Taj Mahal. It was located in a downtown commercial zone, seated about seventy-five, and served curries, rice dishes, and the like for prices that topped out at $12.25.

Donald was opening a casino-hotel called the Trump Taj Mahal. It dominated the skyline in a seaside resort. The multi-million-dollar building contained ten restaurants (none of them Indian), four cocktail lounges, 120,000 square feet of gambling parlor, and 1,250 guest rooms—the most expensive priced at $10,000 a night.

You wouldn't think that anyone could confuse these two establishments, but Victor wasn't so sure. He filed suit for infringement of his registered service mark—and for "unfair competition."

Victor, you don't *own* the name "Taj Mahal," the judge reminded the plaintiff. There are at least twenty-four other restaurants and seventy businesses in the United States using that name. Unless you can prove a likelihood of confusion, this suit is going nowhere. Some of my friends and patrons *are* confused, Victor insisted, at least eight of them. Either they're worried about my links to the Trump empire, or they want me to get them discounts.

Sorry, said the judge. "None of these people actually went to the

*As Donald Trump is familiarly known.

105

Trump Taj Mahal . . . under the mistaken impression that it was related to Victor's restaurant," he noted. As for the unfair competition, that too proved a trumped-up charge. There was "absolutely no evidence," the judge ruled, that Donald had named his casino "with the intention of preying on Victor's commercial reputation."

The Case of the Devilish Lawsuit

You can file suit against the Devil himself and have your day in court, Adolph found, but you won't necessarily get any satisfaction. Adolph filed a civil rights action against "Satan and his staff." The defendant, he claimed, had "on numerous occasions caused him misery" and had "placed deliberate obstacles in his path and caused his downfall."

That might well be, said the judge, but there wasn't anything he could do about it. First, he noted, "we question whether Adolph may obtain personal jurisdiction over the defendant in this judicial district." Nobody knew for sure whether Satan had his legal residence there.

The case might be considered as a class action, the judge went on, but that was going to be tough given the vast size of the "class"—and the question of whether Adolph's claims were representative of everyone else's. Finally, the judge noted, Adolph hadn't given any instructions as to exactly how the U.S. marshal was supposed to serve process on Satan and his servants.

In this case, at least, the Devil came out "not guilty."

The Case of the X-Rated Tax Payment

When she found her property-tax bill in her mailbox, Renee looked at the due date and started to steam. The bill was so late in coming that she barely had time to get her check in before the deadline.

Renee wrote out her $250 check and rushed it to the post office—but she wasn't going to let this pass without comment. On the envelope, instead of "Walter MacKay, County Treasurer," she wrote "Walter MacKay, Bastard."

And on the check itself, Renee used the memo line to jot an explicit two-word message to Walter.

As tax collector, Walter was used to a certain amount of resentment . . . but he wasn't used to the four-letter variety. He filed a libel lawsuit against Renee. For heaven's sake, said Renee's lawyer, can't public officials take a little ribbing once in a while? But the judge was unmoved. The fine he levied on Renee was twice what she'd paid in taxes.

The Case of Life, Liberty, and the Pursuit of Sex

Willard believed he had a God-given "right to sex"—and he was willing to go to court to defend it. He sued the state for having an anti-prostitution law. "Unconstitutional!" Willard cried. He sued the city police for posing female officers as "demimondaines" and luring unsuspecting men. "Entrapment!" he shouted.

The authorities, according to Willard, had forced him into either abstaining from sex or becoming a criminal in order to get it.

When a lower court dismissed Willard's case, he took it to the Court of Appeals. "Patently frivolous!" hooted the Circuit Court. "Devoid of arguable merit." And the judges slapped Willard with double costs and attorneys' fees.

The Case of the Ritzy Toilet Seat

Everyone knew Norm, the plumber, by his family nickname: Ritz. When Norm invented a potty training seat, it was only natural that he name it after himself. He called his toilet seat the "Ritz-Z."

But when that name showed up on the patent applications list, a sharp-eyed attorney hopped to attention. Before he knew it, Norm was facing formal opposition from a most unlikely source: the famed Ritz Hotel in Paris.

The president of the Ritz, who flew to the United States to testify, said Norm had no business using the Ritz name. "The Ritz Hotel in Paris stands for privacy, for perfection, for discretion," he argued. The very thought of a baby's bottom coming in contact with this name—one could only pooh-pooh such a suggestion.

Norm, the plumber, stood his ground. Ritz was "the nickname everybody in the family has had for generations," he said. Besides, said his attorney, "there is such a difference in the channels of trade" of the Ritz Hotel in Paris and Norm's toilet seats that no one could possibly confuse the two.

The Patent Office judge agreed, and he closed the lid on the case.

The Case Against Ronald Reagan

The judge knew it was going to be one of those days the minute he opened Leon's file. Here was a lawsuit overflowing with defendants and claims.

First, there was the matter of Ronald Reagan. Leon was suing Reagan for neglecting him, depriving him of his right to vote,

causing him to be arrested, and bringing about his "civil death." The president, he added, "has acted with redundance and malicious conduct."

Next, there was the matter of Leon's parking tickets. He had stuffed a bunch of these in the file in hopes of getting a jury to help him straighten out his fines.

Then there was the request that someone investigate White Line Fevers From Mars—not, as you might think, a rock band, but a fruit company. Leon claimed W.L.F.F.M. was shipping marijuana, not grapefruit, in its Mother's Day boxes. Leon had lost his trucking license after a run-in while delivering these boxes.

Just to round out the file, Leon threw in a poem he had written about birds, crickets, ants, and a monarch butterfly. The judge also found a U.S. Supreme Court form on which Leon had written, "Why isn't the 1840 mailbox still next to the 1830 one?" and "Something suspicious about that mailbox."

Law school sure hadn't prepared the judge for cases like this one. He figured he would be safe dismissing it as a "frivolous action." But for reasons of its own, an appeals court reversed the case—and there was Leon, back to haunt the judge again.

What the heck? said the judge to himself, and he told his marshals to go ahead and serve process on President Reagan and the rest of the gang. But suddenly, Leon wasn't holding up his end. He didn't return the judge's mail, he let deadlines go by—he "seems to have lost touch with the court, or lost interest, or both," said the judge. And he dismissed Leon v. Reagan for the last time.

10
THREE-PIECE SUITS

■

Cases from the Workplace

The Case of the Rear-Ended Nurse

Nurse Diana had always gotten along famously with Dixie, her supervisor in the emergency room. Famously, that is, until the two joined an eight-day river rafting trip.

It seems that the great outdoors brought out a side of Dixie that nobody saw in the emergency room. She drank like a trooper. She took baths in public. To top things off, she organized a rendition of the song "Moon River" that ended with the singers "mooning"* the audience. Diana said she'd just as soon butt out.

Back at the hospital, Dixie put on her little skit again—and again Diana said no. At this point, Diana started getting bad vibes from her supervisor. Dixie was "harassing her, using abusive language,

*Exposing the buttocks as a prank.

and embarrassing her in front of the other staff." Diana had always gotten high ratings before the trip, but it wasn't long afterward that she found herself jobless.

Diana wasn't about to take this sitting down, and she filed suit. The hospital claimed that since she was an "at will" (non-contract) employee, she could be fired at any time—for "good cause, bad cause, or no cause."

Not so, ruled the court. It was wrong to fire Diana for a bad cause . . . and this case was definitely a bad cause. "We have little expertise in the techniques of mooning," wrote the judge. But "compelled exposure of the bare buttocks on pain of termination," he found, was what the indecent exposure law was there to prevent.

The Case of the Non-Affair

Sick and tired of seeing female co-workers having affairs and getting raises, Bonita filed suit because she *wasn't*. An attorney with the federal government, Bonita claimed her office was an offensive, unfair, and "sexually hostile" work environment for no-nonsense females like herself.

I've only gotten one promotion in five years, though I was eligible for plenty, Bonita pointed out. She also pointed a finger at these supervisors:

• Nick, who had admitted to an ongoing affair with a secretary. The secretary got three promotions, a commendation, and two cash awards.

• Kenneth, who had a "noticeable attraction" to a female attorney. The attorney rose three grade levels in two years.

• Paul, who shared long lunches, dinners, and a resort hotel room with a clerk typist. (According to Paul, they spent the night discussing the typist's "theological problems.") Within a single year, the typist got two promotions, a $300 cash award, and a perfect score on her performance appraisal.

Faced with evidence like that, the court agreed with Bonita. Her managers had "effectively harassed" her, the court found, and she deserved her promotions—as well as retroactive pay increases.

The Case of the Horrible Haircut

Glenn had a vision of the hairstyle he wanted. He had grown his hair out for more than two years in preparation, and—armed with a photo—he arrived at his local hairstyling salon.

When Glenn left the salon, he had a different vision: a $10,000 lawsuit. Gone were nearly 10 inches of his crowning glory, and the ¾ inch that was left amounted to a "ruin." Never mind that the salon offered to pay another hairstylist to "attempt to correct the damage." It couldn't be corrected—there wasn't enough hair left.

Glenn's social life was a wreck. His friends made fun of him "because of the short hair on top of his head and the long hair on the sides." He took to wearing a cap. Finally, Glenn had to call a psychiatrist to treat his "panic anxiety disorder."

In short, Glenn told the judge, he had been "deprived of his right to enjoyment of life" and suffered "permanent and continuing" damages. Spare me, said the judge; it'll grow back. And he dismissed the case.

The Case of the Insulting Computer

Francis was working his way through a new computer program called "Learn To Type Right" when he came to a practice drill that gave him a jolt. It said: "Frankie says noxious things. He writes

118

even worse. He tried to sell us some old junk. Nobody bought it; we wanted good help; sorry Frankie."

To Francis, whose nickname was Frank, this looked a lot like libel—from his very own computer program. He had written "Learn To Type Right." But he certainly hadn't written this paragraph. Francis fired off a letter of complaint to Sizzling Software Inc., the company that had paid him to create the program.

We'll take that part out of future editions, the company promised. And don't worry—no one would recognize "Frankie" as you, anyway. (Apparently an unfriendly co-worker had stuck in the insult.)

Francis was not appeased. He was, as his lawyer pointed out, the only Frank in the credits. He sued Sizzling Software for $6 million. The company decided it didn't want to go to court for libel, and quietly settled the case.

The Case of the Dogged DEA Agent

On a tip, the police grabbed the luggage of Jason, a known drug runner, while he was held over in the airport. They called in the Drug Enforcement Administration.

Warren, the DEA agent, came running, but he didn't have a trained dog handy to sniff the suitcases. So he did the sniffing himself. Sure enough, Warren nosed out the odor of marijuana in two of the valises.

The police nabbed Jason and he was convicted. Jason, however, wasn't about to give in. I never got the chance to test Warren's sense of smell—no fair! he argued. On top of that, he added, the police destroyed the smell of marijuana when they opened the luggage—so the case ought to be dismissed on grounds of destruction of evidence!

Ridiculous, snorted the Appeals Court judge, and he threw Jason out of court. The sharp-nosed Warren, he found, "emerges with his nose unbloodied and his tail wagging."

The Case of the Gaseous Grocer

The two grocery store workers just couldn't seem to get along—you might say there was something in the air between them.

At least, that's what Jeff claimed when he got mad enough to take Marty to court. Jeff's complaint: Marty had "willfully and maliciously inflicted severe mental stress ... by continually, intentionally, and repeatedly passing gas" in Jeff's direction.

Marty had a regular workday routine. He would "seek out" Jeff across the room, and then sidle up to him and take aim. Jeff put up with these salvos for just so long, then decided to fire one of his own. The U.S. courts might have seen $100,000 air-quality lawsuits before, but never one quite like this.

Jeff had some trouble finding a lawyer and finally decided to represent himself. The day of the big blowout arrived, and the courtroom was packed; word about this trial had leaked out. But the plaintiff apparently got cold feet—he never showed up in court.

At that, the judge dismissed the case. He probably would have done the same, Jeff or no. Marty's behavior may have been "juvenile and boorish," said the judge, but there didn't seem to be any law against it.

The Case of the Disappearing Aura

Opal, a professional psychic, should have taken a peek at her own future before going to the hospital for some tests. The contrast dye used in the CAT-scan made me feel "as if my head was going to explode," said Opal, and what's more, the test made my psychic powers disappear!

Before the CAT-scan, Opal had been able to "read auras" around people, predict the future, and hold seances. More than once she had been a psychic mouthpiece for the poet John Milton. Opal not only advised private clients, but she also helped the police solve crimes and find missing persons.

But after the CAT-scan, Opal said, every time she tried to use her

ESP, she got a splitting headache. Finally, she had no choice but to close her office, abandon her career, and call a lawyer.

I sympathize about the headaches, said the judge, but my sympathy only goes so far. He told the jury to make its award solely on the basis of Opal's pain at the time of the test—and to ignore the matter of her loss of powers.

The jury awarded her $600,000 anyway. With the added damages for delay (it was now ten years since the CAT-scan), her total came to almost $1 million. But riches were not in the cards for Opal: The judge's patience went up in a puff of smoke and he threw out the verdict.

The Case of the Dental Evangelist

Tune in a hell-bent preacher on TV and you can flip the channel. Meet him on a street corner and you can cross the street. But when the preacher has got you cornered in the dentist's chair—now, *that's* torture.

Loretta, a dental hygienist, had two callings: her job and her religion. Problem was, she insisted on combining the two. Just when she had her patient nicely trussed up with his mouth full of metal, Loretta would launch into a heartfelt spiel about her religious beliefs.

Bernard, the dentist she worked for, warned her again and again to quit "sharing her faith" this way. It got so that his patients wouldn't go anywhere near Loretta, and Bernard had to do the routine cleaning himself. Six patients left him altogether.

Finally, Bernard had no choice but to fire Loretta—and when she tried to collect unemployment insurance, the authorities said no. At this, Loretta cried foul. All she'd been doing, she said, was exercising her right to free speech.

But Loretta's prayers were lost on the court. She was "behaving against the best interests" of her boss, said the judge, and he was justified when he fired her. "A dentist has the right to expect his hygienist . . . not to add more discomfort to a patient's already uncomfortable situation."

The Case of the Receptionist's Gag

The staff were fond of doughnuts at the doctors' office where Stephanie worked as a part-time receptionist. One day, Stephanie's mid-morning doughnut made her feel queasy.

A co-worker asked if she wanted to lie down or go home, but Stephanie decided to try a method she had used to relieve her upset tummy in the past. She went to the restroom and put a pen down her throat to induce vomiting.

The method didn't work so well that day: Stephanie swallowed the pen. She was whisked to the emergency room, had surgery twice, and couldn't return to work for three weeks. It was when Stephanie filed for workers' compensation that her employers—

and their insurance company—found the case a bit hard to swallow.

Yes, the injury took place during work hours, said the defendants, but you couldn't possibly say it was job related! Yet, that's just what the district judge *did* say, and he gave Stephanie her workers' compensation. But the Appeals Court took it back. "Put-

ting a pen down one's throat in order to induce vomiting to relieve a feeling of nausea experienced after eating a doughnut at work is a risk to which one is not subjected as a receptionist in a doctor's office," ruled the court.

INDEX

Age discrimination, 97
Alimony, 87
"Ambit of danger" rule, 11
Anti-prostitution law, 109
Apology, public, 47–48
Assault, 27–28, 48–49

Battery, 27–28
Breach of contract, 37, 63–65,
    90–91
Breeding, animal, 22–23
Buyer beware, 63

Caveat emptor, 63
Civil rights, 106–107
Class action, 106–107
Constitutional rights violations,
    54–55, 95–96, 98–99
Contract, breach of, 37, 63–65,
    90–91
Copyright infringement, 76–77
Cosmetic surgery, 15

Damages, suing for, 25, 68
    compensation, 22–23, 52
    during construction, 64–65
    funeral expenses, 85
    humiliation/embarrassment, 11
    inadequate tools, 12–13
    loss of potential earnings,
        14–15
    mental suffering and, 24,
        28–29, 45–46, 51–52, 56–57,
        117–118, 121–123
    pain and suffering, 20–21
    personal injuries, 9–15, 26–27,
        34–35, 81, 96–97
    right to sex, 109
Defamation, 47–48, 50, 71–72

Defective and dangerous goods,
    11, 21–22
Discrimination, 56–57, 97
Disruption of the peace, 46–47,
    62–63
Divorce, 33–34, 82–84
    alimony, 87
    property settlement, 86–89

Embezzlement, 88–89
Employment termination, 123

Failure, to submit to breath-
    alcohol test, 35–37
False advertising, 103–104
False arrest, 27–28, 120
Fraud, 64–65

Harassment, 116
Haunted house, 63
Humiliation/embarrassment, 11

Income tax evasion, 104–105
Indecent exposure, 115–116
Infringement
    on copyright, 76–77
    on trademark/trade name,
        53–54, 105–106, 110–111
Inheritance dispute, 19–20

Jokes, practical, 28–29

Libel, 77–78, 108, 118–119

Malicious prosecution, 27–28

Neglect, 111–112
Negligence, 34–35, 37, 51–52
    abandonment of cab and,
        38–39
    during construction, 67
    surgical, 15–16

Nuisance, 61–63, 66

Privacy, invasion of, 73–74
Product liability, 21–22
Professional reputation, injury to, 71–72
Property damages, 40–41, 62–63

Real estate transactions, 63, 66
Reasonable and prudent man defense, 37

Religious preaching, 123
Right to vote, deprivation of, 111–112

Sex discrimination, 56–57, 97
Slander, 71–72, 74–75, 77–78
Smoking rights, 61

Wild animals, harboring, 20–21
Workers' compensation, 124–125

About the Author

K. R. Hobbie is not a lawyer. After getting an irrelevant but enjoyable degree in choral music from Mount Holyoke College, she started her career as a journalist, then lapsed into public relations and business writing. Over the years she has written for dozens of non-profit institutions throughout the United States. The only client who ever argued about her bill (although they did like her work) was a law school.

About the Illustrator

Lucy Corvino began illustrating to alleviate boredom in elementary school. She later attended Rhode Island School of Design, holds a master's in art education from Columbia University, and has worked in the field of museum exhibits. Currently a freelance illustrator, she draws inspiration from the weird people she has met on her travels and the weird pets that cohabit her home.